THE AFTERLIFE OF
J.D. SALINGER

A BEAUTIFUL MESSAGE
FROM BEYOND

CHANNELED BY
JOANNE HELFRICH

NEWWORLDVIEW

NewWorldView
Topanga, California
newworldview.com

Joanne Helfrich
joannehelfrich.com

The Way of Spirit: Teachings of Rose
thewayofspirit.com

Cover Design: Barbara LeVan Fisher
levanfisherdesign.com

Cover Photograph: Tomas Tichy
shutterstock.com

Copyright © 2016 Joanne Helfrich
All rights reserved.

First Printing: May 2016
ISBN: 978-0982812327
10 9 8 7 6 5 4 3 2 1

— CONTENTS —

    Introduction 1

1 I'm still writing 11

2 My spiritual experiences
    after my so-called death 37

3 The purpose for my life 67

4 The reason for writing this book 105

for Paul

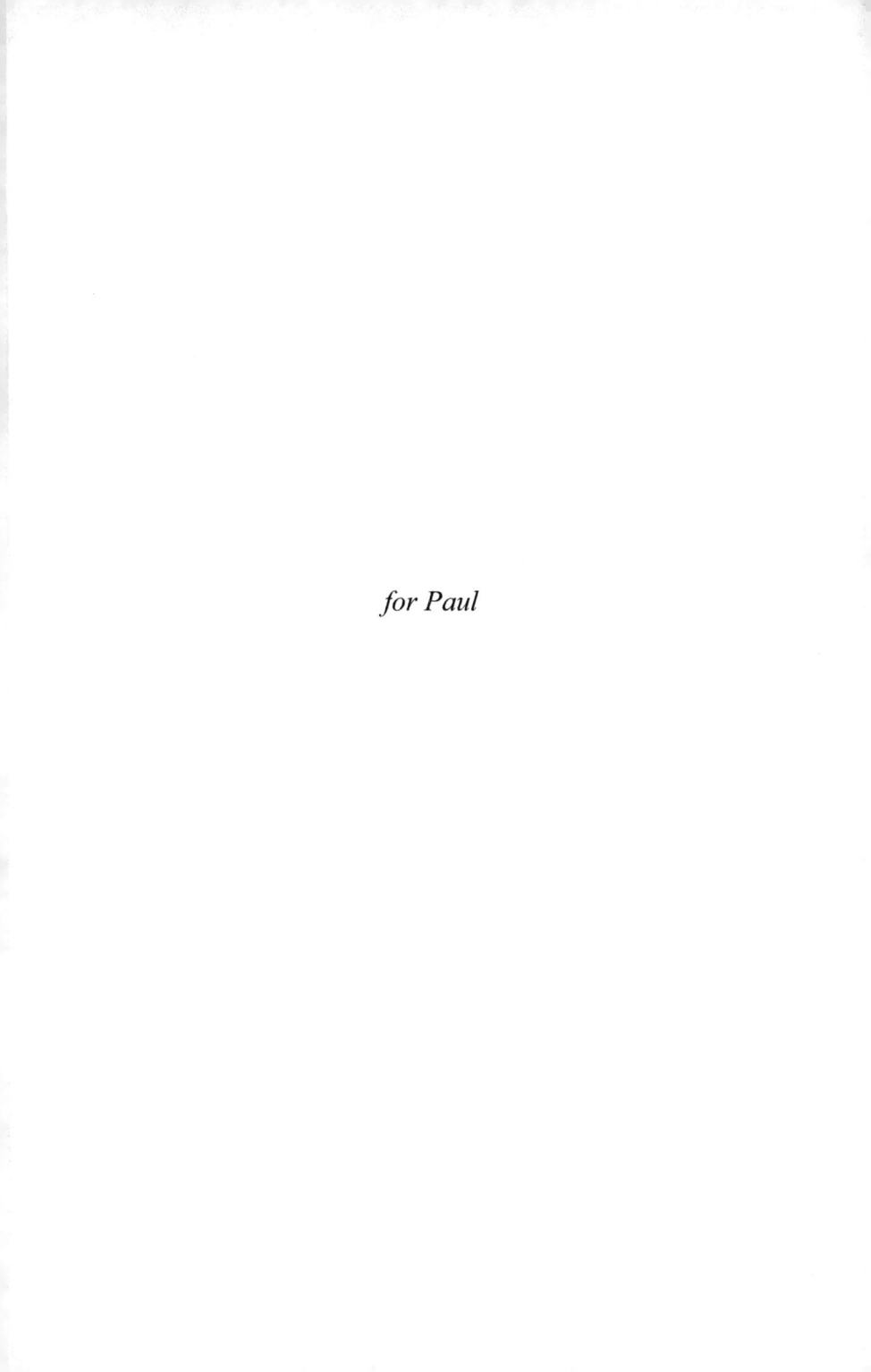

— INTRODUCTION —

> What really knocks me out is a book that, when you're all done reading it, you wish the author that wrote it was a terrific friend of yours and you could call him up on the phone whenever you felt like it. That doesn't happen much, though.
>
> — J.D. Salinger,
> *The Catcher in the Rye*

J.D. Salinger speaks to the souls of millions of readers who love his works. Many of those readers were, like me, lucky to discover *The Catcher in the Rye* and *Franny and Zooey* through our high school reading lists. This is where he has always been needed most—to guide post-world war young

The Afterlife of J.D. Salinger

people, especially, to think independently and meaningfully, to reject inauthenticity, to love deeply, to consider that even the simplest acts of kindness carry in them great divinity.

Of course, few people got a chance to call him up on the phone after reading his books, or at all for that matter. After his giant success with *Catcher*, Salinger moved from Manhattan to a mountaintop in New Hampshire, sequestered himself in privacy, and wrote alone in a bunker-like structure, sometimes for weeks at a time.

He was famously pursued by people wishing to catch a glimpse, a photo, a news story, a bit of advice, usually with the same questions. How are you doing? Are you still writing? Is there anything you'd like to set straight?

He died in 2010 at the age of 91. Now we would never be able to talk to him. Or would we?

In September 2015, I picked up the book *Salinger*, written by David Shields and Shane Salerno. It had been too long since I'd enjoyed anything Salinger, not since the late 1970s when I'd read his other two published books, *Nine Stories* and *Raise High the Roof Beam, Carpenters* and *Seymour: An Introduction*. It was fantastic to feel

Introduction

that I was in his company again and to get to know him a little better through stories about his life.

Jerome David Salinger was raised in affluence in New York City. Drawn to writing and acting, he rejected his father's attempts to bring him into the family business. His writing was forged through his experiences as an infantry soldier, enduring the most brutal combat of World War II: the D-Day invasion at Utah Beach, the Battle of the Hürtgen Forest, the Battle of the Bulge, the final days of the Dachau death camp. It's as if somebody said, "Another hell in the making? Send Salinger!"

He wrote *Catcher* during this time, carrying the manuscript through all those hells, promising its main character, Holden Caulfield—who he always considered as real as anybody—that if he survived, he would someday give Holden voice.

The perspectives of the main characters in Salinger's books and articles reflect his experiences in the war, but are not directly about it. They are extraordinary translations of his experiences into transcendent views of life which, in addition to Holden, are mostly expressed through the enigmatic Glass family, the main characters in many of his short stories and three of his published books.

The Afterlife of J.D. Salinger

There are many personal stories about Salinger: the devastating broken romance with a young woman, and affairs with other—some very young—women, who then felt abandoned. Other people felt abandoned by him, too, including his daughter. Salinger also had a son, who he was on good terms with when he died, as he was with his third and final wife.

There were reports of his having a "stodgy old coot" nature towards the end, defending the terrain of his isolated, ascetic life while seeking his own spiritual liberation. He is said to have left many manuscripts stored in a vault with instructions to publish at specific times after his death.

As any Salinger reader knows, his work is rife with questions (which is something, too, that makes him great). Why did war veteran Seymour Glass shoot himself in his hotel room while his wife slept nearby? Did it have to do with him kissing young Sybil's feet earlier that day, perhaps indicating something sexual? What could Salinger have been thinking when Holden fantasized about shooting somebody, which was what John Lennon's killer—and others who had read *Catcher*—used to explain their violent actions?

Introduction

After finishing the book about him, I wanted to call him up on the phone, of course. How are you doing? Are you still writing? Is there anything you'd like to set straight?

In the 40-or-so-year gap in reading anything Salinger, I was mostly working in the corporate world. I had also started writing fiction, and—with my husband, Paul—explored the work of authors who demonstrated the ability to tap into nonphysical dimensions of reality and report on what they found there. This included, most notably, the extraordinary work of Jane Roberts, and Seth, the "energy personality essence" (perhaps best described as a collection of personalities) who spoke and dictated books through Jane.

Jane authored many of her own books, too, and wrote three of them by psychically tuning into the worldviews of individuals no longer physically focused: Paul Cezanne, William James, and Rembrandt. (My husband chides me on this, but I've never read them.)

In 2007, I discovered that I have unusual psychic abilities, too. By the time I'd read *Salinger*, I had been retired for two years and spent most of my time writing. I had published *The Way of Spirit:*

Teachings of Rose, written by Rose, another self-described energy personality essence. I had also learned to allow individuals who are no longer physical to speak through me.

To do this, I "feel into" specific people or energies, and sense them inwardly and through my hands while I type on my keyboard or speak the words. It's critical that I keep my ego out of the way so they can say what they want, not what I think they would say.

Many of Salinger's themes involve getting ego out of the way, and going beyond it. This was influenced by his interest in Zen Buddhism and Vedanta, a Hindu philosophy based on translations of ancient Sanskrit texts, the Vedas. The Vedas are considered by Hindus to be *apauruṣeya*, meaning "not of a man" or "superhuman."

So in the summer of 2015, I felt that I really might be able to "talk" with Mr. Salinger. However, it scared the hell out of me. For one thing, there was a good chance he really didn't like people doing that.

Another was, what was I trying to accomplish? This required a lot of self-examination. What was my intention? How much was my ego involved with my wanting to do this? Would it get in the way?

Introduction

I had to admit, I would have liked, in the process, to become a better writer. Maybe he could give me some pointers, if he had time. But if he is, as I believed, in a place of no time or space, this would not be an issue, if he had the inclination.

Still, this sort of undertaking is primarily about maintaining the quality of his work, in addition to my own. He was notorious for withholding permission to publish or perform his works if he thought they would be compromised. There are reports that he'd become irate if his articles were even slightly re-edited. Would I be able to get every comma right? Would I do well enough to gain his support for publishing what resulted? How would that work, exactly?

Above all, I was uncomfortable—no, terrified—that pasting "J.D. Salinger" on my book cover might be a good way to sell a lot of books. It's not that I don't want to sell books, it's that making it the goal—allowing myself to be distracted by the potential for success—would cloud the creative process and compromise the work.

If this was my intent, I would know quickly, because my ego would be in the way, and the effort would be doomed from the start. And no one would spot this faster than J.D. Salinger, especially since he'd be, I believed, in my head and heart during the process.

This from *Franny and Zooey*:

> Work done with anxiety about results is far inferior to work done without such anxiety, in the calm of self-surrender. Seek refuge in the knowledge of Brahman. They who work selfishly for results are miserable.
>
> ~ *Bhagavad Gita*

I realized that my intention for trying this was to benefit myself, yes, because how delicious it would be to connect with him! But I also wanted to do it for those who love J.D. Salinger as much as I do, want just as much to know how he's doing, and are open to the idea that this is possible.

There are always people who think this sort of thing is not possible, or is the product of a deluded mind—*mine*, that is—but I decided that's okay, because I'm not doing it for them. Realizing that this may benefit

Introduction

me *and* others, and not caring so much about what some people may think, helped me break through this challenge.

Then I did what anybody does when they want to talk to somebody they don't know: I wrote him a letter. I didn't send a physical letter, of course, I stashed it away. But it made it into the book, at a specific place, at Salinger's prompting.

This book is a response to the letter and my inner contents at the time it was delivered over the course of four days in September 2015. You'll see that the beginning is directed more to me personally than the majority of it, which is directed towards you, the reader. You'll also notice a shift between "I" and "we" at some point. This is not an error. It is explained as you read on.

The text is exactly as it came through, with minor edits to correct the words I didn't get right the first time, and to add punctuation and section breaks. I also asked for, and received, a few clarifying sentences where I thought they were needed.

The four section titles are verbatim quotes from the text they represent. I think he had this in mind from the beginning because the manuscript broke so

The Afterlife of J.D. Salinger

easily into these four pieces, which correspond nicely with the four Vedas.

Yes, it seems to me to be written Mr. Salinger. I know for sure that *I* didn't write it, that I was only the transcriber who for practical purposes assigns my name as author. You can decide for yourself.

In any case, I hope you find value. I have, and I'm also very grateful. In addition to all the beautiful things expressed herein, finding his voice has helped me find mine.

When he died, Salinger's family shared this:

> His body is gone, but the family hopes that he is still with those he loves, whether they are religious or historical figures, personal friends or fictional characters.

I think this is exactly where he is now. I hope you do, too.

Joanne Helfrich
Topanga, California
October 2015

— 1 —

I'M STILL WRITING

The first thing to realize is that I am not only still alive, I have doubts about how I will make this compromised state of writing work for me. There's a sort of translation that is required for both myself and the person hearing my thoughts, which in this case is you, Mrs. Helfrich.

I hope I can answer both your direct as well as indirect questions, which you have in mind when you think about me. The way to consider this is perhaps something of a mindfulness, meaning your mind and mine are full with each other's thoughts.

The way to consider this, too, perhaps, is a dance that you and I will do together to soften each other's personal thinking about the "right" way to think and dance so that we can effortlessly glide across the floor with the best of what each thinks helping us along. Like Fred and Ginger, only with less showing off and more obstinate thoughts, at least from my point of view.

The facts are that there is no death, that we go on living as we did before, and that I have many friends who care about me still. I know this because I had them when I was living, not so much now because the world is very different for me.

The purpose is to write, period. It does not matter whether you write from my perspective or yours which, by the way, is increasingly suspect if you start hanging out with writers like me.

I have no compunction for telling you to stay alert for mistakes, such as more words than required, and clichés. My hatred for clichés is renown, as well as fighting too hard to be heard. It's not so much that you need to be heard, it's that you have to be heartfelt with what you say. This is the key to writing well. You cannot have any fear about not writing well if you just say what's in your heart.

So let's get on with this message to the world about how I am doing, because I daresay they will

I'm Still Writing

want to read my thoughts as to how I'm projecting outward into the cosmos now, with pen in hand.

I'm still writing. The factual world was one sort of Promised Land of writing for me, as a friend of mankind who disliked any sorts of conflict, much less military conflict. I have spoken from the depths of my soul, on occasion writing from a heart which was severely broken in my twenties, first by a girl, then by a nation—that is, a national disaster.

The purpose for writing is always to express what depths of emotion are there in you, whether you survive a war or not. The path for many was to die, the path for me was to live beyond the years that were truly painful. They were all painful in one way or another, whether in writing or salvaging what little I had with regard to my feelings, instincts, separation from those I loved, and the many forms of outsidedness that I explored while alive.

It wasn't so much that I cared for people and then abandoned them. I cared for them and then had only myself to be salvaging my emotions from the place of pure agony that I felt in my teens as well as twenties. I chose a path that respected my experiences enough to transform them into something that was livid with rage, while expressing also the soft belly that we call our love for self and others. In this, I was not going to flinch. It was all I could stand to take in what I had, then put it out in forms that were not only readable but evoked a greater sense of urgency about war.

The wars were horrendous. I was not a good soldier. I was a dense kid with too many literary ambitions to succeed in helping anybody at the time. This sense of guilt was part of my pain: I did not do enough for others.

This was perhaps the main problem I had with changing roles into adulthood. I knew I had let people down, knew I had grasped too much with my writing it all down, translating as I went through even the worst crimes of war. It was all I could do to survive with my heart intact. That heart suffered so, and now I see that was not only something that I did that was heroic, but I am also engaged with healing those parts of me that have had to—strange as it sounds—be whole again without the world looking in on me.

The face I showed to the public was not my true face. The true face is what I wear now. I am happy, healthy, more or less given over to love for myself in ways that I had not learned before. I'm not saying I

I'm still writing

I AM HAPPY,
HEALTHY, MORE OR LESS
GIVEN OVER TO LOVE FOR
MYSELF IN WAYS THAT I HAD
NOT LEARNED
BEFORE.

had anyone to blame for being born as a man in the worst place on earth to learn yogic practices, but because I was, I had always hoped to be a better practitioner of it. That said, there's no reason anybody can't love self, given the many things I had to hate myself for.

The path for many is influenced by the corporate structures that too often weight down the experience of love and life to the point of damaging each individual that comes in proximity to it. The damage can be small or not small, in the case of your experiences.

For example, you are now reacting more than responding to the patient humming of your writer's life. You have not really gained much from the corporate world. You have friends there still, perhaps. You need love for self to get you through the phase you're in. Heaping praise on you is not needed, for you have reason to feel great about where you've arrived, because you've lived through a war yourself. It's not that you have needed to fight as

I'M STILL WRITING

much as surrender to the corporate world. You've done a good job of preserving who you are, learning from your lesser soldiers, too.

The soldiers are all around you. The point is, you're all soldiers, beaten sometimes by life, crazy from war, learned from experiences that sound wonderful (Hürtgen Forest, doesn't that sound delightful?). Yet in all your gory meetings you stand up for self and God when you say things like, "I love others. I need others. I crave your company." Even those small habits of life can make a bit of crap turn out to be paradise.

These lessons I had not quite learned when I was alive. I shied from others, mainly because I was just shy. Spoken word was never my strength—writing was. So when I felt that I could not retreat quickly enough or completely enough as the years went by, I simply didn't want to talk to anybody.

Imagine that. With all your spurious devices that chatter, even without someone talking at the other end of the phone, you can't really get closer to yourself. Do you see? I had to take aim at that whole notion of the chatter of life. That was my main reason for the seclusion.

The Afterlife of J.D. Salinger

In this capacity for being quiet, that's where the magic lies. It's where creation happens—true creation—which is the most beautiful thing in the world as well as beyond it.

The creations I had connected with—and I mean that most sincerely, I did not create the Glass family or Holden Caulfield or any of the nuances they brought with them so marvelously—I was not the writer for. I was the conduit only. There was something or somebody else who wrote these books. I was good at picking up on these things, these people who I love so very desperately that I gave my whole life to them.

The fears that people have in engaging these sorts of dearly creative acts have to do with the ego self. The ego gets in the way, simply put. The ego doesn't like to think there are many others around who want to help. The ego doesn't like that one bit. So the ego says, "Well, I will go up on a mountain top and make hay with writing." It will say, "I will turn out a large manuscript," or whatever you want to make it.

I'M STILL WRITING

THE CREATIONS
I HAD CONNECTED WITH…
I WAS NOT THE WRITER FOR.
I WAS THE CONDUIT
ONLY.

The Afterlife of J.D. Salinger

However grand the notion of this, the ego will rebel, too, at having to do this all alone. It will feel badly about having to suffer through the pain of creation, the spurning of other activities to devote their time to the craft. In fact, they will be so at odds about this that they will reason that they are not only the warriors, but they are also the enemy.

Do you see how the ego plays out in the world? How desperate one becomes by allowing this sort of ego-driven life to succeed?

I spent nearly six decades on a mountain in New Hampshire. I lost so much in the process: friends, lovers, children. I can't describe to you how much I hurt them. I hurt myself, too. The ego was harmful in the sense I could not read into my spiritual direction the need for the living people in my life. I knew ego needed to be integrated, loved into my core of myself. However, I had such a hard time with that. The fears were that I would not be loved by anybody. The fears made themselves real when I was in the bunker, alone with my ego, but also with somebody else: my Wholeness.

I was there with my Wholeness in the sense of my ego being able to hold it together enough to allow the great Self to come through me—all of me—

I'm Still Writing

through my many aspects of selfhood, through the Glass family, through Seymour, especially, who guided the whole thing.

Getting to that place of pure connection was the goal. However I needed to do this, I needed to do this. I suffered for it, my family suffered for it, and I was not afraid in the sense I knew I needed to write write write. That's all I lived for. I promised that I would write. I did that. That was my gift to the world.

This sounds totally ego-bound, but it was not intended to be that, because the ego did not produce it. J.D. Salinger did not produce it. The Glass family produced it. The team of creative intellectuals, bright beyond their years, significantly loving to each other and to the world: they wrote the books.

Holden was a cousin of sorts who—which pleases me still—had to let down his guard to be the soldier that he was. He was not sufficiently brave, he was sufficiently surrenderable. That was his aim, that's what he accomplished. The path for him was not so much to fight for what others fought for, but to surrender to the idea that his way was not to go theirs.

Holden guided postwar America through the tunnels of salvation by suggesting to them they would not be anybody at all should they continue to do what they did. He suggested to the world that to fight was the answer—to fight from the heart and soul for one's independence from vulgarity, from stupidity, from anything that reeked of inauthenticity.

The facts remain that Holden did not succumb to the world: he fought it with his every breath. What better role model for young people than somebody who has the nerve to say what he really thinks? You all want to take aim at people sometimes, don't you?

Now, there's something that I did to make this more of a problem than it should have been. I did not intentionally include passages in Holden's story that were meant for an out-of-balance individual to kill anybody, or even potentially hurt somebody. This was never my intention. My intention was merely to say, "Who are you really taking aim at? Are you taking aim at our brothers overseas in countries that you don't even know where they are, geographically speaking? Or are you taking aim at the individuals

I'M STILL WRITING

WHAT BETTER
ROLE MODEL FOR YOUNG
PEOPLE THAN SOMEBODY
WHO HAS THE NERVE TO SAY
WHAT HE REALLY
THINKS?

who are purposefully taking aim at you through their actions of greed and hatred and inauthenticity? Which, by the way, is the root of the problem?"

The inauthenticity problem is one that suggests that you don't really know what you're talking about. The inauthenticity problem is the ego being all tied up in how he looks and acts. It's the purposeful life that dies in the process, the one that says, "I can't do this on my own. I need to have friends in the earthly world and friends in the spiritual world," (I'll get to that) "and I will not be told what to do by those who sacrifice nothing for anybody."

That's the problem with inauthenticity. It is not what it's cracked up to be. It's the bane of civilization. That's why Holden wanted to take aim at somebody. It's just a way to transmit the idea that you are not only *not* getting the full story from people who want to rule you, you may need to consider taking them on, even violently perhaps. For why would you not do so if your family's survival was on the line?

Now, this is not to say I am pro-violence. I'm not. This is only something that needed to be included in the book very briefly.

I'M STILL WRITING

In fact, Seymour himself succumbed to the pain of sacrifice as well as non-sacrifice. He could not deal with the inauthenticity of himself marrying somebody who was typically American, who had no idea of what an authentic life would even look like when she saw it in Seymour. He reasoned, badly perhaps, that if she could not see even the smallest bit of the irony of postwar America still wrapped up in the bonds of full inauthenticity, then she'd see it after he shot himself in the room they shared.

It was an awful thing to do to her. It was a shallow thing to do in some ways, too, because there was never any doubt that she appreciated him for who he was. She loved him. Yet he could not stand the pain of knowing there will never be another life beyond war. There never is. You can save all the people you want to, and God knows, many die trying. But there's no real life after war for very many veterans. There was no life after war for Seymour either. The realization that he would never really heal is why he chose to die.

The Afterlife of J.D. Salinger

This is not to say every soldier dies when he is in war—spiritually, that is. He dies after the war, mostly returning home now, getting his due with regard to benefits. Having injury that has made life difficult is another way that soldiers suffer. These are all psychic wounds, whether they are physical or not.

The depth of pain in soldiers who serve on the front lines is inconceivable to people who don't go there themselves. There's suffering so great that it would make you crazy, and that's happening, too, all the time. Every person you send to war comes back a little insane. Take that to heart. This is in spite of all the political grandstanding that occurs. That just makes it ten times worse. And in history, you will see how each day that is spent in war is a day that growth and beauty do not occur. It is hell, and it is something that needs to end soon for the sake of all people, not just this country's.

So in the spirit of my continual haranguing that I do in my books, I will offer these suggestions for ending wars.

First, don't do it.

Next, if you do it, end it right away.

Then don't do it again. Period.

I'm still writing

EVERY PERSON
YOU SEND TO WAR
COMES BACK A LITTLE
INSANE. TAKE THAT TO
HEART.

The Afterlife of J.D. Salinger

The reasons for war are only to protect one's self and those they love from harm. That's not what's going on now. What's going on now is an atrophy of spiritual connectedness that engages only the worst in people, men mostly. The women aren't off scott-free either. They tend to push soldiers along, too, sometimes, because they see this as so glorious.

The afterlife being what it is according to those individuals who see jihad as affirmation of a great afterlife: that's nonsense. You go as you. You take with you all the shit that you learned and all the problems that you had. You will get a lot better view of a heaven if you treat others with respect while on earth. The only way to get to heaven is to be heavenly.

The jihadists don't know this. They come back to haunt spaces they died in, a lot of times, because they can't let go of the war. They can't let go of the violence. They don't do the work needed to let go of the ego, either. And what you have, therefore, is just a cluster of abomination that precludes much spiritual learning for a time. Then some get the idea that they are wrong for doing these horrific arts. They go into a sort of coma of violence, they see what this is to others, they learn from it. The coma incorporates enough tolerance of others to realize the suffering that's endured by the violence.

This is the preferred way of some people: to go into a space of coma-like tolerance that helps them see what the results of their terrible actions are. They realize they will not be happy doing this any longer. They choose to go beyond this in the afterlife. That's what they do. They are not surrounded by many virgins and wonderful things right away. They need to move beyond where they were first.

This is a giant leap of faith to think this way: that we have an afterlife that's very similar to our physical reality. This is also perhaps the best change in belief structures that one might ever imagine.

I can speak from authority on the subject because I am now in the afterlife doing what I do, still writing. I can't tell you how glad I am that this is happening. There are no words to describe it.

The Afterlife of J.D. Salinger

This sounds odd coming from somebody who writes for a living—still, in a sense—however, it's really unfathomable. There's nothing to do all day except write. The way to think about this, perhaps, is that I don't really know who's writing anymore, just as I can't really know who's reading it. The purpose I guess is to have fun doing what I do without need to worry too much about it.

I realize now that people will do what they will with the books I'm writing. Yes, they are books. This is my favorite form of writing. The purpose for my doing this is just to do it the same as I did when I was alive, or tried to.

The thing is with being physical: it's really a challenge. The way people go about doing things always has some measure of need in it. They need to do things to write, such as create a bunker, in my case. This was something I needed to do to preserve my sanity because there wasn't anybody else besides the characters in my writing.

The reasons for doing this in this way were, as I mentioned previously, that I did not really need anything except the writing, or so I thought. I was trying to move beyond ego needs. This was a mistake, as I also mentioned earlier, that the ego self needs to be realized fully into a state of grace, you might say. So I confused the ego with something badly flawed and evil, even. This was not the correct path to take.

The Vedanta religious view is that somebody up there wants you to be whole, yes, because that's Godness, in its mightiest form: Whole. But the means to do so in Vedanta are not going to always be creating the best person in the process of doing that.

The person that I was trying to be was somebody who was cleansed of all evil. That was what I thought. This was not practical because I was not cleaner, I was just solitary. This is not to say I did anything wrong. I don't feel that I did, but the reality is that my solitude was not always having the effects of goodness in my life. The extremes—the hiding, the diet, the emancipation (or so I thought) from reality—were not practical. In fact, this was not even healthy to some degree. So I was not perfectly following a spiritual path, if there is such a thing, but I did my best.

Sages will tell you that to love others is the best way to create a happy life. This is potentially the best path to salvation, too. If you truly feel bad about what the world has done to you, and what you've done to the world, the best thing to do is to love somebody. That's always true. The somebody that you love needs to be you, at least.

The part where it gets tricky is in accepting who we are. I feel very accepting of who I was, much more than I did when alive. I did my best. I know that there were things I can do better and I am doing those now. So the afterlife is very healing in that respect. I can turn things around here in ways that I didn't when I was physical.

I was saying earlier that the physical world has some boundaries to full expression because of the needs we have to do certain things before we can write, such as eating, drinking, and so on. The purpose to all this is not to hamper creativity, though this is something that I didn't see. The purpose is to do what you do every day without worrying too much about anything.

I wrote a lot when I was physical. There are manuscripts ready to be published during intervals that I have specified, so my work will continue,

I'm Still Writing

IF YOU TRULY
FEEL BAD ABOUT WHAT
THE WORLD HAS DONE TO YOU,
AND WHAT YOU'VE DONE TO THE
WORLD, THE BEST THING
TO DO IS TO LOVE
SOMEBODY.

The Afterlife of J.D. Salinger

physically speaking. However, due to how I now see things, I can also be writing from beyond the tomb, as it were—beyond the tomb of that bunker that I occupied for so very many years.

In fact, there's sort of a bunker around me now. I have created a sort of paradise here made up of friends who love me, family who love as well as hate me (we will get to that), and the stormy weather of New Hampshire. I loved the storms most of all.

The paradise I now occupy includes the sort of bunker that has always worked for me so well. Fireplace, table, chair, windows, etc. The path away from the bunker leads to the house, as it always did. The sparse weeds around the path are still here. The fields, the trees, the valleys of my beloved home are all here, too.

There are not many people around to bother me and discourage me from writing. I felt all along that people were trying to discourage me from writing by talking which, again, I was not as inclined to do. So it's a more peaceful place where the masses, as I thought of them, are not really interested in going to. In fact, they hardly come around at all. In this respect, I sort of miss them.

I'M STILL WRITING

The family has some bearing on this paradise, of course, and I don't want to speculate on how they feel about me now. There are many people that I love who I did not treat well all the time, and that's a fault of mine.

However, I do maintain that I have needs that were also unmet by some family members, so they aren't particularly well represented in my new world. I love them still. I wish them everything they could want, and am sure they are getting exactly what they need for their own growth in the afterlife and in physical reality, too.

— 2 —

MY SPIRITUAL EXPERIENCES AFTER MY SO-CALLED DEATH

Reality is so very occupied with love that you can't really see it when you're physical. It's as if the fluidity is arrested or frozen, and the love has to work harder to be visibly impressed upon what you see and hear and perceive at all.

The reason I tell you this is because when you go to your own private heaven—or hell, as the case may be—you don't realize it right away. You carry on as if you're everybody's friend, father, or writer, as in my case. I was not at all ready for what I found there, in spite of what I thought. I did not at all feel ready to go in some ways. I felt that there would be a giant light that would just immolate me physically and I would leave the planet in a state of blissful healing.

REALITY IS SO
VERY OCCUPIED WITH
LOVE THAT YOU CAN'T
REALLY SEE IT WHEN
YOU'RE PHYSICAL.

My Spiritual Experiences After My So-Called Death

I realized I needed to heal some things. That was clear. I was always aware that I had some reasons to be healed in spiritual ways, mostly. However, there was never any reason to believe—based on my teachings that I loved so dearly—that I would be anything but blazing with spiritual truth. The way I saw this was as an acceptance, as well as surrender to God.

The right way was to get there through cleansing spiritually as well as physically. Therefore, that's all I did in my later years, cleansing myself of spiritual needs, physical needs, while writing my observations about the Glass family, who in every way embodied who I wanted to be—as well as be *with*—forever.

The same practices that I use are those that many others use in getting past the ego into a state of joy caused by complete solidarity with God. However, the path always has stumps in it, and weeds and things that require one's attention. This is something I lacked awareness of, and in this, the stumps grew into whole trees that kept me from realizing the goodness all around me. The trees were examples of things along my path that I needed to review, the way I treated others that were hurt by my actions. This is not to say I didn't try. However, I did need to see things from their perspective.

The trees were in so very many ways captors for me. How lovely to be held captive by trees. Yet the path of illumination was, therefore, beyond something I needed to get past. The trees helped me to see things more clearly.

The forest of trees was something like the Hürtgen Forest, alive with vitality of Godhood while immersed in the blood and guts of soldiers both German and American. The Hürtgen Forest, therefore, because of my experiences there, became the most perfectly fitting metaphor for my spiritual experiences after my so-called death. This was something I didn't even think to imagine. The path for me would always be a burst of fire, then immersion.

However, the forest provided me the perfect path in which to see beyond the trees, which I climbed with great speed, only to find at the top the immensity of all of Creation. The path towards heaven, the path towards hell, are all included in that

My Spiritual Experiences After My So-Called Death

Great Forest. The reasons for my wanting to see beyond it were perfectly simple: I just needed to see the sun again.

Having experienced the forest in my waking physical life, I did not accept this at first as my solitary path to spiritual life beyond the physical one.

There has always been a part of me that loved that forest, however brutal it was for everybody who went there. This was perhaps the single most effective device I had to access my inner emotional state and take in whatever I could to transfer it to paper through my intense intellect. The intensity was needed in order for me to translate that. Emotionally, I would not have made it.

The path was all about my intellect resting on my emotions as a sword, with which I could penetrate the everyday drama and pierce the veil of separation that was my intellectual meanderings about some people who were not even really there. Holden Caulfield, and the Glass family, and everybody who inhabited my stories were all ready to be with me if I was able to use my sword to carry forth my mission through that hideously awful experience I had in the forest.

The Afterlife of J.D. Salinger

This said, there it was again for my use in getting beyond it. The path was not so bleak if you could assume a higher ground. How apt a metaphor for my life beyond this one: seeing above the trees of the Hürtgen Forest, past the concentration camps and Normandy beaches, beyond the pain I was causing myself and my loved ones still (in my thoughts), and beyond what I thought of as the sunny Godhead, who was really just the sunshine of my own thoughts about it.

The path was always there, I just didn't see it as certainly as I did until after I died.

Now, you may be thinking that I was not deserving of an award as an actor, but indeed I was: when I was alive, that is. I was finally the actor I wanted to be in my later years, not the same way I thought I would be in my earlier years as an actor in my school days. I was not perfectly attenuated to the sort of acting that others did. I was gawky, stumbling over words sometimes, not fittingly handsome in some ways, adoring of acting as a pastime, not so

MY SPIRITUAL EXPERIENCES
AFTER MY SO-CALLED DEATH

THE PATH
WAS ALWAYS THERE,
I JUST DIDN'T SEE IT AS
CERTAINLY AS I DID UNTIL
AFTER I DIED.

much a career. And what I learned there was that people really do have a lot of reason to own up to who they are.

Acting is, generally speaking, being a phony. It's something that you do to practice being a phony in your own life, too. Often this is what games the system: you get to be the phony you always thought you were, and people respect that about you.

However, the phoniness isn't just there, it's everywhere. It's in the supermarkets, for example, when you try to buy something that you think is good for you because somebody else told you in an advertisement to get it, when in reality you didn't really want it. There's reason to question even these sorts of things.

But the way I saw acting was, I could step outside myself. I unlearned this in the war. I was not able to step outside myself in the sense of phoniness, that is. What I was able to do was to step outside myself in response to the suffering that I—Jerry—was experiencing, and what I stepped into was the Glass family.

I was having second thoughts about acting while I was in it, and thought for a while that I was just too odd a person to do it. That was my basic idea about

My Spiritual Experiences
After My So-Called Death

myself: I'm just odd. I was half Jewish, Park Avenue bred, sophisticated beyond my years in some ways, truly not mature with regard to women, and pained by having a testicle that refused to enter the picture. The solidarity I had to do my writing was informed by all these things. You don't have to show anybody anything that you don't want to.

This is not the same for acting, when you show what you need to show to get the idea across that you really are the person you're intimating, or perhaps even embodying. Lots of people do this—actors—they embody people fully, and that's what I did in the war. I learned to be somebody else, whole families of people. That's where I got my stories. That's why I survived the war.

From the spotlight of the stage I learned nothing except to inhabit somebody else. From the glare of war I learned to be many different people—from Seymour, who was perhaps most like me, to Holden, who was war-ravaged yet still innocent, to even Bessie, who was not somebody I took lightly, but learned to infuse in her and many of my other characters a light, of sorts, a reason for being in the world, a state of being that was delightfully luminous.

The Afterlife of J.D. Salinger

When I killed Seymour, it was not to put out his light, you see, it was to illuminate others through his works. Seymour died to enable others to share his light around with those they loved. In this way, I was able to infuse my own writing with that of a justifiably damaged yet insightful-beyond-his-years man who needed to go. He needed to move onto the next phase, Seymour did. That's all that was about.

In his defense of shooting himself in his hotel suite, the way he did this was to call attention to his pain. He would not have done so desperate an action if he had not been in so much pain. This was not something that he needed to do for spiritual redemption, to kill himself, however.

He suffered from the same pain I did and felt the same as when I returned from war: I wanted to die. However, I lived differently. Seymour had no way to do this. He had tried to force along a marriage that was doomed while nursing a soft spot for the youth that was in peril, the innocent child that was represented by Sybil.

MY SPIRITUAL EXPERIENCES
AFTER MY SO-CALLED DEATH

SEYMOUR DIED

TO ENABLE OTHERS TO SHARE

HIS LIGHT AROUND WITH

THOSE THEY

LOVED.

Seymour was not only fraught with pain, he was also forced to look at something that he did not want to see: his perpetual anger at the world. He was angry, Seymour was, and he could not realize salvation without doing something to break that anger. Sybil was the best token that love had to offer him. He knew that God had sent her his way. He knew Sybil was there to save him from his anger and pain. Her voice is the voice of God.

Anybody who reads this as sexual innuendo is missing the point, halfway at least. That Sybil is a child who he kisses on the feet has nothing to do with his own sexual feelings about women in general or lovers who may be young. This is about kissing the feet of his Savior—his love for life—which are the same things.

The anger was not pent up anymore, but what he did not realize in effecting that shift of his anger was that his reasoning brought into his awareness the basic reality that he could not live anymore. There was no way he could reconcile his anger, which was perhaps even worse now that he was with this innocent child who would eventually be corrupted or even shipped off to war. This was too hard to imagine. So he realized that, rather than spending his

My Spiritual Experiences After My So-Called Death

life with the anger, he would end it in hopes that he would be spending more time with his goodness, with Sybil representing his divine child—his wise child—in a space that would allow that, as his current situation did not.

※

There is no feeling worse than not knowing what you want to do with your life. It's a stranglehold on one's thoughts like nothing else. Nothing else will do because the path is initiated by love for life, period. Nothing takes the place of that.

The reason Seymour got his path loused up with fear is that he did not consider that he might actually have a path ahead that was not going to damage anybody, including himself. There's not anything in the world that could have stopped him then. He was bright—considerately so—and game for anything that would have allowed him peace. But he couldn't fathom doing anything that would potentially hurt somebody. If you think you don't hurt somebody at least once a day, you're fooling yourself.

THERE IS NO
FEELING WORSE THAN
NOT KNOWING WHAT YOU
WANT TO DO WITH
YOUR LIFE.

My spiritual experiences after my so-called death

That's why Seymour had to go. He did not want to be the person who accidentally stepped on somebody's feelings in the effort to do something good.

It's not why he got loused up, though. He got loused up on his path because he needed something better to do than to sit around hotel rooms with his newly born wife, and by that I mean her innocence was too much for him, too. Granted, there were people who could have helped him get a book deal, for example. That would have been something for him to do, because he was a writer, of course. But the path was not certain in the respect that he could not fathom getting anything done without harming somebody.

The path, therefore, was fraught with too many challenges, too many beautiful weeds along the way to his salvation. So the only thing he could do was to do what he did: take his life to the next place. There's enough pain and suffering in the world to choke anybody setting out to do anything worthwhile. That's why Seymour had so much conflict: he didn't see his future.

The Afterlife of J.D. Salinger

Now I am where he is. I have a future here, I realize that. I'm not really dead, though. I am so not dead you wouldn't believe it. The way I see this situation is that I am finding out how to realize nonsuffering in ways I couldn't when I was breathing air like you are now.

There's a sense of breath here, not like anything else, though. It's as if something has come into your lungs that's not only perfectly clean, it's vitalizing in ways that are pristinely comforting to oneself. It's as if somebody has taken a breath that you breathe, too, and they, in the process, take away all doubt and fear.

The purpose of this is certainly benefitting me, as I am continually feeling better and better about everything. The path for me was not something that most people take on. I know I abstained from more than I needed to. In some ways, I potentiated disease of my mind. I was not a happy person.

The breath now is so very important. Every cell of my body is feeling great. Now that I am nonphysical, breath has turned into a sort of love burst that slowly filters through my system and cleanses me. It's something of a situation of healing that is thoroughly enjoyable.

My spiritual experiences after my so-called death

When I was alive on the earth, I forget now what caused this, but I had a sharp pain under my right thigh that was not healing. This is now healed, my body is stronger, and I am enjoying walking more than I did. The effortlessness of walking is coming back.

In this situation, I devote most of my time to writing, of course. Walking is second. Tennis is in the works. There's nothing better than knowing that the path is free again to enjoy. See what I mean?

It's never going to end, either. The path is going to go along its way forever and you will be on it forever. So you might as well enjoy it now because there's no turning back or realizing anything except that you will enjoy it most of the time. The other times will be fraught with changes because you are a soul in process, but that is going to be all right because there are always going to be people there to help you. If there aren't people, there will be angels. Of course, sometimes these are the same things.

※

In my devotion to Vedanta, I sought something that I should not have been seeking, that is, cleansing of my soul. This was a dangerous notion to have, and one that was not only physically discomforting but emotionally discomforting, too. The path is not for getting onto then running. The path is for getting onto and enjoying. The path is your path. Mine was not completely sane in some ways. The path is not ever supposed to bring you into a state of feeling that you have to get so much better than you are.

The way I see this now is that I felt guilty about some of the things I had done in the war. I did not want to kill people. I did have to because they were killing me and my friends, or trying to.

The purpose for war, therefore, is monstrous. It's as if you can't really do anything except suffer along with every other person there in spite of whatever you were before and after the war happened. I was so very terrible at it that I wonder how I survived. But I realize now that it's only because of Holden Caulfield. Holden saved my life. He was the reason I succeeded in not dying in the war: so I could share him with others.

The suffering, though, was so great that I had no reason to feel especially guilty about asking, then receiving, a sort of penance for it. The penance was to write solidly for the rest of my life. This penance

MY SPIRITUAL EXPERIENCES
AFTER MY SO-CALLED DEATH

THE PATH IS NOT
EVER SUPPOSED TO BRING YOU
INTO A STATE OF FEELING THAT
YOU HAVE TO GET SO MUCH
BETTER THAN YOU ARE.

was joyfully accepted. What I did not consider, though, was that in the real world, you can't just go into a bunker and stay there forever with the idea that everybody is going to just need you for that.

There's something to be learned from this, and that is that you don't exist without others. Your purpose is to be who you are, yes, because that's how you were born and live and die—as a solo act. Because that's how you adapt to life and grow spiritually—as a solo *condition*, though, more than a person. The condition is fairly simple to understand.

You have a reason to die, too, as much as you do to live. So why would you not do this in ways that benefit others?

The condition, therefore, is how you get past yourself, and *your* condition is how you do that in the world. The condition is how you treat others, because they have to deal with that condition, too. They respond with their condition, and over and over again.

My Spiritual Experiences After My So-Called Death

You get the sense that life is all about not really being a whole person, but a nuanced set of expectations and purpose. The nuances include: what did you do as a child? What were your parents like? There are skillions of times that I've looked at myself in the mirror and thought, "Well, who the hell do you think you are?" That's exactly the condition, it's who we *think* we are—not so much who we say we are or who we pose as—that really gets to the heart of the matter.

The person I thought I was was not a solo act as much as he was a solo expectation of something that was grand, when the reality was, he was not something—anything—like that. He was somebody who just didn't know what to do with anybody. That's a condition that others had to learn from and place in their own sets of expectations and purposes for their own requirements.

The set of expectations I had fit perfectly with those I knew. The women, especially, sought somebody who was not going to treat them well. They did not expect that. That was their condition. The path we walked together was like a puzzle, going from one end of it to the other, all fitting together on each side with paddle-like pieces forming intricate designs. They were stunned to realize that I was not the person I thought I was. Hence, the condition snuck up on them, as conditions always do.

There's no cure for conditions except the cleansing of one's fears. I mistakenly thought this had to do with the cleansing of one's soul. These are not exactly the same thing. The fears are something I'm still working on.

The soul is always going to need somebody with a condition like mine to be perfectly happy doing what the soul does: learning and growing into maturity. The soul always has reason to be perfect. However, the soul—intentionally—does not always do things that are perfect. The soul is always perfectly imperfect. That's what the soul does so fantastically well.

The reason I have to tell you all this is because this is part of my healing of my condition. I am more than Holden Caulfield, more than Seymour Glass, more than J.D. Salinger now. I am all of that and all the lifetimes I have been through, and am still going through, too. There's no eternal soul that does not constantly have existences forever and ever. That's what makes them souls. They exist in eternal life, and there's no eternal life without existence in it.

MY SPIRITUAL EXPERIENCES
AFTER MY SO-CALLED DEATH

THE SOUL
IS ALWAYS PERFECTLY
IMPERFECT. THAT'S
WHAT THE SOUL DOES SO
FANTASTICALLY
WELL.

The Afterlife of J.D. Salinger

The path I have chosen incorporates so many more people in it that I can't even tell you how many. They exist in a sort of "life code place," if you can fathom that. The life code place has a secret door to it that you can get through with the gate key, or code, that you sense. Does that make sense?

The reason I'm telling you this is because that's what's going on now with this book writing we're doing. The reason I exist in these pages has to do with the fact that there's somebody who senses my gate code and has the desire and will to make sure that the words I say get onto paper. This is what I do now, too. I write books and I have no reason to stop doing that.

The purpose for this sort of engagement of the writer of this book is to help me do what I want to do, and this corresponds very well with what she wants to do—indeed, seeks deeply to do. What she wants to do is to extend my knowledge into the written works that you are reading now. What is something of a challenge is knowing the codes to the

My Spiritual Experiences After My So-Called Death

locks on the gates. This is not something that is rational, it's all about how it feels to her. This is exactly what happens when you realize that you're not really a person, you're a condition.

Now, I have spent many years in my lifetimes thinking about this. How would you know that if you didn't see that there are reasons to want to explore this sort of thing? Why would you not want to find out about what happens after you die?

This is her condition, and maybe you have it, too. This is not to say you have any reason to, though. That's the point. You don't, but if you have—or *are* that condition, more specifically—you would not need to question that. You would just want to unlock the gate with the code. That's why you're who you are. You need things others don't. You're a piece of the grand puzzle and you don't really even have to think about it.

※

That's why I got fouled up. I thought about this too much. I was thinking that there was only one way to live. The Vedanta religion was it, baby. It was more than I could handle, though.

The purpose to any religion is to be a better person. This is good and well-suited for people who have the condition that they really need to be a person who is better than what they were before. So they go forth into the world bringing cheer and love and life to many. This is a good condition to have because there's so much benefit to this. The condition is a healthy, wonderful one.

This condition is what I sought, really. I needed to be a better person. Somehow, though, people get turned around and they don't consider that the best way to be a better person is to treat others better. This is what I didn't realize. I thought I needed to eat better, or slim down more, or have more privacy than I really wanted. In fact, there's no negating that I didn't want to cause suffering, hence the aloneness.

Yet there's also a factor involved in any situation like mine and that is that sometimes religious thinking has you tied up in the belief that there's a rodent in each of us that needs killing. This is preposterous because rodents, even, have their place in the world. So you try to kill the rodent in you, when the reality is that you need to be friends with

My Spiritual Experiences After My So-Called Death

the beautiful creature who is so sadly misunderstood. You need to engage it to say, "I know you have reasons for being here. I want to help you be who you need to be, too. You can't just go around infesting my life with your little nests, though. So I will take you lovingly into a space where you can thrive and have nests of joy in your beautiful space."

That's all there is to it: the beasts in us all have reason to live. So I took this poor little mouse of a person—this terrible little, sore, bruised mouse—and I did not accept that he was somewhat beautiful, too. I despised him instead. That led to my total breakdown in the post-war weeks and my total, longer, slow descent into sorrow that followed my return to the States. The path for me wasn't so much about loving the rodent as much as loving the best parts of myself as well, not feeling persecuted, not feeling that the path for me would extend into anything other than bliss.

The path for me led to a bunker in which I spent too many days suffering, yet in the long run I needed to do. This is not Vedanta so much as a Zen way of looking at things: that you need to suffer through some things in the best ways you know how, and I did that. I sought to comfort others through my pain, and that's what I did right.

What I am getting to, though, in the sense of my longing to be better, is that I suffered more and I made others suffer more. That's not what I would do again. It's not what I would suggest, either, for anybody else.

Vedanta has its place in the world. It's the oldest religion by far, the set course for us humans, and I mean that because I still have humanness about me in the eternal world we all share. The Vedas are the most beautiful things to me still. They are the best teachings by far that I have ever seen.

The purpose for religion, based on what I have seen, is good. The limitations we have with dealing with our inner little wild beast is something that is very necessary. The Vedas teach that if you have a demon inside you, that you need to be rid of it, however. This is not accurate. The demons need to be loved. That's what I got wrong.

The reason for this is, of course, that there's no such thing as a demon. This is simply a condition that needs healing. The Vedas do not exactly say this—

MY SPIRITUAL EXPERIENCES
AFTER MY SO-CALLED DEATH

THE VEDAS
TEACH THAT IF YOU HAVE
A DEMON INSIDE YOU, THAT YOU
NEED TO BE RID OF IT… THIS IS
NOT ACCURATE.
THE DEMONS NEED TO
BE LOVED.

they don't say "exorcize the demon"—they nudge one into considering the release of the demons. In my view, this is something of the same thing. But what I realized in the process is that I was telling the more selfish little beast in me to simply go away, when I should have been loving it to death.

The Vedas, therefore, are of the most benign and helpful religious texts there are, much better than those that say "exorcise your demons." Therefore, they are the best that I have found. The problem for me was, "How will they be interpreted and lived?" That's what I got wrong.

— 3 —

THE PURPOSE FOR MY LIFE

This is something that I truly want to set straight. Because I was not going to give up on the Vedas, I incorporated more of the not-really-true aspects of what I was learning.

The beast in me was decidedly male. I wanted to purge my maleness. In fact, I was so very purging of my maleness that my femaleness suffered.

There's no point in going on about this except to say that the purging of one's femaleness has to do with the maleness in each of us. When you consider how brutal men are, you sense there's a reason for it. That reason sometimes has to do with gold, with profits, with corporate interests. In the operating systems of each device that you now use, there's profit involved. When profits go too far into the space where there's a real problem with being kind to each other, that's greed: the greed that I felt had everything to do with the male domains of success.

Reality, therefore, was in every way intruding on my female space. That was why I took up with young women. There was not a perfect solution to the problem of how my inner maleness was threatened. The problem was definitely beyond my scope of reasoning, inhabiting all the spaces in the world.

The purpose for my life was to get some balance between male and female, each one having a say in matters both personal and prophetic. The reason I say "personal" is because there were times I really felt that the suffering was all going to end with a giant explosion that would blow up the earth and I was powerless to do anything. The prophetic part is that I was reasonably sure that my work would help others see that war was not going to solve anything at all, and that the female aspects of earthly life were the

THE PURPOSE FOR MY LIFE WAS TO GET SOME BALANCE BETWEEN MALE AND FEMALE, EACH ONE HAVING A SAY IN MATTERS BOTH PERSONAL AND PROPHETIC.

most important things, as they were the things that were loving, respectful of life, guiding others towards a full-out, making love sort of experience that was revealed later on in the sixties with the potential to go farther, too.

The male, therefore, was not exceedingly strong in getting my life—my personal life—in order, nor did I reason that this would have much effect on the world. That was my feeling at the time when I was able to coerce women, and I do mean that specifically. I was a famous author, after all. Coerce women into needing something from me. I was therefore doing exactly what I hated about men: taking over the world. I did not see that at the time.

The fact that I was able to coerce them so easily had me thinking that I was the wrong one. They were not, most of the time. Sometimes I was not as kind as I could have been to women, either. However grand my notions of feeling that I was successful, they were not the people I needed them to be, either, which was strong.

Do you see? Their vulnerability made me so freakishly scared of life that I ended up shunning them after I had taken them over. This was what I said at the time: that they were not fraught with

The Purpose for My Life

enough strength to be worthy of my love. That's not what I know now. What I know now is that they were exactly the right people for me at the time.

This is going to the Zen place again. Of course they were the right people at the time, even though I did not realize it at the time. They were not the right people, too, in the fact that they were not strong enough to take my point of view enough, or to say, "It's not going to work with me, this daddy thing that you have going on. It's going to need some balance in this relationship or I will not stand for it."

The way I see this now is that they were absolutely right with everything they did to help me. They were very maternal. They were very needy, too, in the reasons they chose me, which was to get support from me in the male sense. So it was a set of conditions. We all have them. Again, that there was learning that occurred—by both letting go of the fear that they were not fully whole on their own, and for me, learning that people really do not require anything other than love—is the point.

The point that I desperately want to make, though, is that they were everything they needed to be: not less than, not weak, not at all inferior to me. They were my equals. I did not see that, and in many situations they were exactly the heroes they needed to be. They were strong, they were agile on their feet, with this old body skulking around. They were lovely, independently secure, more than they considered, perhaps. The way I see this now is they needed something from me that was not what they thought, and that was strength to do what they were going to do without needing anybody else's permission to do so: not God, daddy, anybody.

So that's what I think needs to be said for femaleness all over the world: you have the strength that moves mountains. Don't ever forget that.

Female energy is what Holden was also tapping into. The reason he left school was to form his own self without needing the permission of anybody at all, even his own sets of expectations. He was given to the school in the same sort of sacrament that many people do when they offer up their children to college life. It's the same all over the world, offering up one's sons and daughters to the machine called corporate interests, and painful wars. Ultimate

THE PURPOSE FOR MY LIFE

WHAT I THINK
NEEDS TO BE SAID FOR
FEMALENESS ALL OVER THE
WORLD: YOU HAVE THE
STRENGTH THAT MOVES
MOUNTAINS.

sacrifice is the point that we say, "Okay, that's all I can do."

I am saying now without any hesitation: there's not any reason to sacrifice our sons and daughters to war. There are no expectations, in spite of what you think about God, that He needs you to send your sons and daughters to meat grinders like those of the Hürtgen Forest. The way you have of thinking about religion is that it guides you to do God's will, and I'm telling you this right now, from my more informed perspective, that there's no reason to believe this.

Would God really want your sons and daughters to watch their brethren get eaten alive by mosquitos, much less by a round of bullets? Would you really think that was their best, most happy and spiritual path if they could choose one? Do you really think anybody really wants to see even their own enemy die before their eyes, especially if you're the one who drove a sabre or bullet through his skull, his heart, his abdomen? Is there any sense in this at all, except to fulfill the obligations of total domination by those who wish to drive out anybody who has an opinion other than theirs?

The Purpose for My Life

The answer, it seems, is the reason I wrote these books, and still write these books, and might go on forever writing these books. The purpose for life is to enjoy it—that's all I ever wanted to say in my books—and to enjoy it, you need to sometimes walk away from the life you've been taught is the right one for you, which is what Holden Caulfield did. The reason he walked is that he saw the path ahead as stupid, ignorant, and full of fear. The reason he walked was to show others how you can do that, too.

That's why I write books now, too. There are ways to walk away from life when life is not what you want it to be. Here's how.

Like Holden, you have free will. There's not anything special about this except that you don't need to listen to anybody except yourself. That's what he does.

Next, find a path for you that helps you bring joy to yourself and others. Do this in that order: self and others.

Next, find a reasonable way to live among others without compromising your values of freedom and peace. Let go of expectations that there's some paradise waiting for you somewhere if you can only be a better person. This is the tripe of religion that guides people into wars. Don't believe it. The reason to find ways to live among people is they make you better people if you let them. Try to do that.

Next, the purpose for your life, as I said, is to enjoy it. Take down anybody who says otherwise by saying, "That's not the case, to live in fear." Take on the people. Don't shoot them, just say, "It's not going to get any better if you keep insisting people are bad." Enjoy yourself. (The shooting has a place, just not nearly as much—*not ever nearly as much*—as you might think. The people who have guns are fearful that they won't go to heaven because they're so evil. Don't believe this.) Everybody has a condition—*is* a condition—that you can work through with others.

Next, I can't begin to tell you how great it is to know that life will continue eternally. There's only one thing to say about this and that is free yourself from the thinking that you will not be held accountable for your actions. You will be, only it's you who will do that, not some God who strikes down sinners. No such thing has ever been true, ever.

THE PURPOSE FOR MY LIFE

EVERYBODY
HAS A CONDITION—*IS*
A CONDITION—THAT YOU
CAN WORK THROUGH
WITH OTHERS.

The Afterlife of J.D. Salinger

When you think that, just say to yourself, "I am loved and will always be loved," and I can't say enough how true this is.

There's never anybody who is alone. You can't perhaps see this now because that's what you chose for your life, but I can see this is true now in my space, which is what I will talk about now.

※

The many lifetimes that we share all have to do with getting through the pain of life together. There's no one who ever is alone, ever. The reason for this is that you have in you a bounty of individuals who claim to know what you need to know in any given situation, and *do* because they are also you in other lifetimes.

This may sound weird to say, "they claim to know you," because this is not the case. They *do* know you intimately well, they have known you intimately well for many, many years and lifetimes and whole armies of lifetimes, but you think their claims are just that: *claims*. You have learned to distrust your own inner authority, when in reality,

The Purpose for My Life

they know much more than anybody. They have the best insights into your particular conditions that you might ever imagine.

This is the key to this wonderful journey you're on: you are more than you imagine. When you think about how I learned about life, you get a sense that the fictional characters in my books were invented by me, but you will not believe how much they invented *me* until I tell you.

Think about the process by which you have an army of people going to war. You have recruitment efforts, you have induction ceremonies, you have uniforms, parades, marches, then go off to war and kill people or be killed. In my world, this was always a giant problem, of course, and it is in yours.

What if these people who inhabit the army of your choice were actually fighting *for you* all the time? What if they had the experience and desire to only serve you in particular? What if they were there to escape death, and live for the moment, and for you? They would do what? Put down their fears, their guns, their lives, even, for one purpose and that was to help you do what you do.

Now imagine this peaceful army of total strangers helping you with everyday things. What would they do? They would, foremost, say to you, "I'm here for you. I have knowledge that you might use for yourself or others." You might have them dress appropriately, such as in colorful clothing. They might wear what they wanted to wear, depending on their own particular position in life, or their own sense of style, or as a reasonable way to get through their own lives and help themselves to grow spiritually. What they would look like is however you think the entire planet looks like forever.

Do you follow? You have an army of individuals at your disposal to help you do what you need to do in your life. The only reason to sometimes say, "I ask for your help," is when you need to, that's all. They don't direct your life, they don't ask you for anything except to be happy. How is that for an army? Wouldn't that be great?

The fact of the matter is that you have this all around you all the time. The army comes clothed as dogs, cats, trees, lovers, pagans, churchgoers, informed introverts, silly extroverts—any range of person you might imagine has in them the ability to assist you. How's that for a different way to see armies?

THE PURPOSE FOR MY LIFE

YOU HAVE AN
ARMY OF INDIVIDUALS AT
YOUR DISPOSAL TO HELP YOU DO
WHAT YOU NEED TO DO
IN YOUR LIFE.

The Afterlife of J.D. Salinger

How grand to know there are more people who want to help in some way than those who want to harm others. The harming isn't always harmful—though that's getting into more of a Zen place than we want to go into right now—but suffering is really needed at times because it helps you to become more compassionate towards others, and that's what you need to realize sometimes, too. The path for you has many challenges, and the path can be very steep, but knowing that you're loved eternally is going to help you.

That's why we still write books now. The reason we live is to help others. I have my conditions—in fact, I am a big condition, as we said. My big condition self loves yours into the next reasonable space if you let me. The way I see you is that you have a gift that you can eventually help me with, as well as fun to have ahead that will someday be my fun, and probably is now because all things exist all at once. This takes a bit of getting used to because there's not any evidence of this, but it's not at all bad to think this now.

The Purpose for My Life

When you decide to check out of the Hotel Earth, you will find this to be true, and perhaps you may want to express your support for my work when you see me, because I will not be the sort of convalescing soldier that I was before. I am much more apt to say hello. Just don't keep me from my writing for too long, that's all.

※

In the respect of my writing, I have lots of things going on. The books I wrote will come out in time. They are sealed in a vault now, and will have people trying like heck to get them out at reasonable junctures so as to be enjoyed, perhaps even in your lifetime. This is why I timed them this way, sensing that the world is changing, and I will know better in the future what others need to realize.

The fact of the matter is, I'm writing them now. When I say that I was predicting the future and how my work will effect this, I was tuning into this focus of attention now, this pattern of atoms that is not quite physical yet duly impressed with enough form to move around, do things, get coffee, etc. These are not patterns like you have ever seen because they exist without the spectrum of light that you are used to seeing.

So in my departure from your world, I left behind patterns of productive work that transcended a bit into what I'm doing now. The patterns are formed by consciousness. I have some reason to continue writing, and although I'm not doing this on earth, I will always do this here. The patterns form microatoms, you might say, that go beyond physical reality. The books are part of this pattern of microatoms for which I include my basic longings from here now, which I can instruct others on in the future, for the future is not set, it's here now. All of it is here now.

When I say that I'm writing *for* the future, I'm writing *in* the future. The books I'm writing are the same books that will be published later—in *your* later, not *my* later, because there is no "later" in my world. The fact that you believe in a "later" says you're going to be physical. The world I inhabit has both "laters" and "all nows." So in my laters are your books, because I'm sentient enough to say, "That's for later, that's time-based." That's enough for me, to sense the future, to be part of that future.

THE PURPOSE FOR MY LIFE

THERE IS
NO "LATER" IN
MY WORLD.

The Afterlife of J.D. Salinger

So this is a bit complicated sounding because it's sort of impossible to explain, but I exist in the future, the past, the eternal now, and it all depends on what focus I choose that things happen. That's all there really is to it. Simple, huh?

The way I have of tracking the future, past, etc., has to do with my gauge of what's possible. See how that might influence you, too? Do you see how perhaps if you were to think something is possible that it actually might turn out that way? See how when you consider, for example, how Holden saw things in the future, that that's what happened?

※

When I wrote the book, *The Catcher in the Rye*, I was certain that Holden could see the future. There's no turning back from the future that you're creating as long as you believe intensely that will happen. Holden was the sort of fellow that could express that future well. He had the gift. He had the particular strengths, as well, to say, "I'm not going there."

THE PURPOSE FOR MY LIFE

The past for him was in many ways unsupported by truth. It was something of an aspect that he had reasoned away as something that was coldly dead to him. The future was only something he might choose, at that point, that had no bearing on the past, which, as we said, was dead. He knew, therefore, that the past is only an invention, as surely as the future is.

This is another point we want to make: that you only have the present moment to have fun in or help somebody or whatever. There's no future or past in our line of thinking now. It's just that you create it for your own purposes because that's how you think, but the reality is there's no need to fear either the past or future. It's that fear that you have all the time that keeps you stuck. The unstuckness is in freeing yourself from the worries you have about everything, that's all.

Reason has reasons (sorry) to be, surely. However, reason is not the only thing in your bailiwick of talents. You have also the courage to be non-reasonable sometimes. Taking hold of your internal thoughts has to do with how you feel—and we mean *feel*—because you have no reason to adopt the idea that you are merely problematic,

The Afterlife of J.D. Salinger

programmable robots, to hold onto versions of yourself that you foresee will be super-fantastic in the future. This is not the way life really works. It's really about how you hold onto how you are inside, without feeling you have no reason to exist.

There's no such thing as reason, when you really consider it. Reason goes along with what you feel. Otherwise what would you have? Fear. You would just keep on fearing that you have a sort of place in the world that you need to protect, and an identity to protect, and that's not how it really is. You have no identity: you're a condition.

This is something of an unusual way to think, we realize: that you have a condition, you are a condition, etc. But think about how liberating it is to think that you're more than what you feel, even. What about how great the world is to you? How about the world being what you identify with? That's what you came here to learn, and is something I have learned, too, as well as strive to educate others about.

That's how I have fun now: educating others through fiction. My sort of condition is about that. How's yours now? What is it that you feel strongly about? Do that every day, in every moment. That's how you can have fun most of the time.

The Purpose for My Life

WHAT IS IT THAT YOU FEEL STRONGLY ABOUT? DO THAT EVERY DAY, IN EVERY MOMENT.

The Afterlife of J.D. Salinger

The set of conditions that I call mine are "A Savior of the Planet" now. This is not something to take lightly, nor is it something new. We all have things we want to save. However, "savior" isn't exactly the right word for this. It's really about being free to be who you are, rather than trying to save anybody. When you consider yourself a savior, you get all hung up on others.

The thing to realize is that the saving part is really about saving your love for the things that matter: the trees, the birds, the sky, the glorious things around you. That's what matters. You're on a beautiful collision course with joy if you just think of all of it as you. That's why you're a savior. It's all you, buddy. The worms, the mice, the cheese, all of it. That's so beautiful, isn't it?

You'll see how very easy it is to love the things that matter when you get past your fears about who you've been taught you're supposed to be. Your very nature is imbued with all of creation. The purpose for your life, therefore, is to just be who you are. That's all you need to do.

The Purpose for My Life

The way we had of getting past our fears was to just do what we wanted to do and that's all we did—the Glass family, the Caulfields, everybody we ever knew and loved. The reason we are saying "we" is that I'm all that now. J.D. Salinger is officially part of the family now, if there was ever any doubt that's where I lived most of the time.

The reason I say "we" now is to help explain what really happened in all those bunkers in the war, and in my home. I was protecting myself from the experience of singularity, which is the worst way to live.

Singularity is the number one reason people kill each other. They think they are the only thing in their identity, when the reality is that all people are one. And if you kill somebody, for example, you kill yourself. And in my view of the world, I needed to protect myself from the view that I was all that, I was not ever *only* J.D. Salinger. I knew deep down about this multiplurality, I will call it, this version of life that unfolds into itself, that incorporates many others.

The Afterlife of J.D. Salinger

I hid from the world so I could be all of them—all of the families of the world, in some respects. I reached into those areas of consciousness to entrap the enemy: the enemy of fear and doubt about the real reason for living, which is to love. I had to go about it in an odd way, however. That's all I did all day, was join my friends in their Manhattan apartments and New Hampshire abodes when in reality—in this reality—I was never there physically at all.

How could I write about them if I hadn't experienced them individually as a person who was physical? Because if I had, I would have been disappointed they had not any of the conditions I needed to say what I needed to say to the many families who needed those conditions in order to surrender to faith that all things really are good.

The reason for my hiding was that I had to objectively pursue this without distraction. This was all going on inside me all the time. I had to write it down. This was not my doing, it was theirs, all of them, every family who had a child in danger. I had to say, "Stop this. There is a better way." For the lives of the children going off to war, I had to intervene through Holden to teach them that this is a better way.

THE PURPOSE FOR MY LIFE

FOR THE LIVES OF
THE CHILDREN GOING OFF
TO WAR, I HAD TO INTERVENE
THROUGH HOLDEN TO TEACH
THEM THAT THIS IS A
BETTER WAY.

The Afterlife of J.D. Salinger

What a sense of responsibility I had, and although I was game for it, not everybody—at least in their ego selves—were, and that was difficult for everybody.

Now, when the ego gets involved, all hell can break loose, though sometimes it's okay because the ego needs to be in charge of some things. Letting people do their thing is important. However, when ego takes charge of others, that's when the hell occurs, and in the sense of my own destiny, I had an ego that really needed to go beyond where it went, trying to help others around me be better people. I had no clue as to how this would occur, really. If they didn't read the books, then so what?

That was my calling: the books. When I intervened into their personal space, I was challenged by my own ego, as well as theirs, and could not escape except to my writing. This caused a lot of damage to my own ego and theirs. What the world had for me ahead was to grow up a bit more than I could do on earth.

The Purpose for My Life

So my ego had nothing to do with my passing, although you may think yours does. You want to give up the ghost sometimes. However, mine didn't want to go without some sort of cleansing ritual and that, as I said earlier, was not the point.

This was where Vedanta failed me, or at least those who translated it badly. This occurs in almost every religion, though, so this is not to slam Vedanta, only to say that you really need to be careful about what you believe.

The first rule of Vedanta is to be in the world. This is all about being the person that you are.

The next is to form family wherever you can find it.

The next is to take up a cause. The third is perhaps the one that most people avoid because they are stuck in an embrace of wealth and fear that is harmful. So this is something people don't do easily sometimes.

The next is somewhat of a phase of renunciation that comes with the loss of faculties, such as physical infirmities, etc. This is not to say this has to be done because of infirmity. It's really about letting go of physical reality. This is not something most people do when they can instead deny away anything that seems like passing on.

This is also something people have a hard time doing, so much that every funeral parlor in the world has some degree of denial of death, of not really embracing death. It's a big business, these funeral parlors. Don't give them more business than you need to.

Let go of whatever you can while you're alive. Don't fear anything. For me, I needed to do more letting go, perhaps, than I did. I said I would write until I died, and that's not really taking leave of something. In fact, this was pretty much clinging to what I'd found to be satisfying. Great people—unlike me—know when to quit. This was something that I felt I could do while I was around and I did not really feel like stopping. Getting older doesn't mean you need to stop what you love doing, it's just that you do it with less concern about how it turns out. That's the difference. So letting go of the devices that I did to (mistakenly, perhaps) ensure good books

THE PURPOSE FOR MY LIFE

LET GO OF
WHATEVER YOU
CAN WHILE YOU'RE
ALIVE. DON'T FEAR
ANYTHING.

was something I could have let go of: the nervousness, the solitude to some degree, the tics I had when producing work. It was not something that you needed to be around. You could sense it in stories about me. I was alone much of the time and was paralleling the world, not in it. So it was being fully alive while also living in a tomb, not something that Vedanta would suggest.

This is how I came to be in the world and not of it: theatre. Theatre was something I'd always loved very much, not so much to act, because that's not something I did well, but to write for people in the way they actually are. Theatre allows people to break out of their shells a bit, venture into new chemistry around and through them, and sharpen their ability to deal with chaos in things, like improvisation, and doing things in the crafts of service—lighting, building sets, etc. Each part is a whole that makes something very beautiful. I loved theatre for this reason, and because I really loved being somebody different for a while.

The Purpose for My Life

When I died, I had two choices. One was to predict what next future focus—lifetime—I wanted to have (and I did not realize at the time there were such things as past focuses I could go into, but that's another story). The other was to go to my ex-life and relive what I needed to. I did not want to relive my life. I wanted to go beyond life, so I did not feel completely at ease with the future focus idea, either. I wanted to do what I was doing when I died.

The purpose for this phase is to make sure you know what you're doing so you can grow through it, to evolve. For when you go, when you die, you don't stop growing, you don't stop evolving. There's little doubt that life goes on after you die and the soul does not perish. I know this firsthand. There's every reason to keep going, after all, because that's why we love life—we don't know what to expect, we want things to be easier.

So when I was asked by an energy that I can't really describe well (except to say this was a loving soul, older in some ways than I, younger too), I felt that I did not want either choice. So I sent some psychic energy to the personality who was asking the question that specified "I'd like to choose from some more options."

THE AFTERLIFE OF J.D. SALINGER

THERE'S LITTLE DOUBT THAT LIFE GOES ON AFTER YOU DIE AND THE SOUL DOES NOT PERISH. I KNOW THIS FIRSTHAND.

The Purpose for My Life

He or she (it was uncertain which gender he was, although in this forum of souls, you might say, all beings are neither male nor female; this is a broader topic that I will only summarize as needing to let go a bit of your gender assignations) said, "Well, what do you want to do?"

I said, "Keep doing what I'm doing."

She/He said, "You can't do that until you have a sense of what you're doing that's in need of knowing."

So I said, "Well, I'd like it to be more fun and less work, perhaps. I'd like to ensure all my characters are safe and alive somewhere, too. I'd like to know they are fine."

That's when the very floor underneath my feet dropped down several hundred yards, and in the process, I let go of a lot. The spot that I landed on was a stage. It was a proscenium arch that I stood on, looking into a sea of nonphysical faces. The audience was comprised of all my physical focuses—from all my lifetimes—looking at me with rapture.

They wanted me to take a bow. I was not feeling up to it. There was writing to be done. I needed time to work out some things. I wanted to do things in my way. They had other ideas.

The Afterlife of J.D. Salinger

What was so entrancing about this scene is they really did want me to take a bow. There was no fighting it. This was a sort of curtain call for my life. I sat down and looked at them. I couldn't say a word. I was thunderstruck with the knowledge that I really was admired and appreciated. I couldn't have guessed that, I really couldn't.

※

You might think I was very sure of myself all through my life because I was successful and had a home in New Hampshire that I escaped to. For many people, that's something they want to accomplish.

However, there was never any need to feel a sense of accomplishment. To me, I needed to continually write. I was obsessed with it, and for good reason: it was indeed my calling. However, in the making of books I forgot one thing and that was to let myself enjoy every single second. It was always about working out this train of thought or that page of details. I was never really satisfied. I needed to feel satisfied, and the best way to feel satisfied is to receive the sort of love and admiration that I got that

The Purpose for My Life

day, that nondual day on the stage in front of my peers, my peers of soulful personality that were all me.

When you get to the point that you seek admiration, do this: just sink into whatever space you're in and allow the love of God, or others, whoever you want to think about, let them embrace you and applaud your efforts. They all know you like the book that you are. They love you for everything that you have done, good and bad. They need to have you know that. Let them.

Finally, I stood up and took a bow. There were tears in my eyes that I had never really had in that way before. I was able to go back to writing with a totally different view of things. Instead of feeling that I had to do this writing thing because I needed to help people, I knew I was already doing that.

Just the action of sitting down to try to help somebody or being out on the street, however you do that, even that is a joyous act. You don't have to publish books to have that feeling. You just need to realize there's an army in your corner wherever you go, and that's all they need to know to love you: that you are trying. Indeed, what else can we do?

— 4 —

THE REASON FOR WRITING THIS BOOK

The reason for writing this book here—this one, by this talented writer in her own right—is to help her, too. She has reasons to be who she is, writing these books from another dimension, you might say. She has purpose to her life. There's not any reason for her to have bad feelings about whether this comes out in stores or not. She is doing her best. The reason she has this gift is because she allows it only. That's all anybody ever needs to do to accomplish nearly everything they are drawn to.

The fact that she has reason to want to do this is the point: she loves it. There's happiness in every one of her microatoms and loving thoughts for her every time she enjoys herself. In this way, she fulfills her destiny. Does it matter if she is ever a successful writer, master of her own domain, angelic in action in every motion, surveyor of the fields of God with not enough equipment to track it all? Not in any way. The reason she is doing this is that it's fun.

Here's another reason. When you have something that you want to do, there's always somebody who wants to do it with you. Now, these can be good things or evil things, to be sure. However, when you get past the idea that doing evil things is fun, you'll really get the best of what life has to offer. When you do good things for people, you get a whole world of army people standing in line wanting to assist you.

She has a similar love for the same sorts of things I do. In fact, she and I share very big characteristics, as some of you do with her and I as well. The thing that may be different is that she has a very simple plan for accessing the people she wants to: she listens with her heart.

The fact of the matter is, she fell in love with my writing, not with me. The sense of proportion of herself to the Universe grew as a result. The purpose for this was the same as it was for me: to grow into

The Reason for Writing This Book

the sort of person who would want to play in these worlds together. That's what we're doing. When you get lost, when you find out that you have suffered way too much, you can sense energy around you that has an effect that is truly remarkable. They are always around you.

She did not require any training to connect with me. She needed only to ask.

※

Here's her letter.

Dear Mr. Salinger,

I enjoy your writing very much, and enjoy reading about you. I am also a writer and live a somewhat isolated life, with my husband and two cats. My interests are also in the mystical, and I have some experience in speaking with those nonphysical, which is why I'm writing to you. (Even though you won't get this in paper form, there's something about being clear in one's intent

The Afterlife of J.D. Salinger

that is important to me, and I sense that you will get this letter in some way, perhaps through my own eyes.)

This may seem misguided or even insane to some people, such as your biographers, who wrote that you "sought to exit the world into a purely meta-physical realm. But this didn't succeed, it can never succeed, because we are flesh-and-blood beings."

I don't believe that. I believe, as you once wrote, that "we're not… persons at all, but susceptible to myriad penalties for thinking we're persons and minds."

Would you like to try to correspond? I welcome your thoughts and perceptions on your current arrangements, and anything you'd like to share with any readers we might have. If this experiment works, I would like to publish the text, whatever the length, with your permission.

Best wishes,
Joanne Helfrich
Topanga, California
September 2015

THE REASON FOR WRITING THIS BOOK

This elegant little, wantonly bold, crazy as batshit letter, which was written with no expectation that her addressee would even have eyes to read it, got me to the quick. I have never received a letter like this, nor will I ever for as long as I'm no longer physical.

The fact is that this is the most unique sort of letter I've ever hoped to imagine, and in this, she was the agent of great musings on what sorts of parables I would tell through her fingers (she writes with her eyes closed, feeling her way into my soul). The fact that she asked me so kindly and with so much respect had so much to do with why I decided to take up the challenge.

What would happen if she didn't do this as well as I would have liked? She would not have published it. She specified in her letter that I would give her permission. Although this was not anything that would realistically hold up in a court of law, it was heartfelt and real. It was also what was required for engaging somebody who she did not know.

The Afterlife of J.D. Salinger

When you engage others, you have a sense about them that has more to do with feeling than it does anything else. You feel people. You "get" people or you don't. Sometimes you develop strong feelings for people, and as a result you fall in love. The reason you fall in love hasn't anything to do with looks or values. It's feeling.

In your plane of existence, life abounds full of love, even though you don't really feel it all the time. This is in many ways due to the fact that there are many different sorts of feeling tone, and this gets into why I love her letter. Feeling tone is what you would call the deepest way to really get into something or someone.

Everybody has a tone that you can feel into, like the gates that we discussed earlier. The gates or passages are unlocked when you realize how to push those things open without any kind of effort: the code is all that's needed.

In your feeling tone, you have others who feel like you do, or feel like each other do, and that's called simpatico feeling. We are simpatico—she and I—and you are, too, if you've read this far. Do you sense others are more simpatico with you than others? Yes you do, and there's purpose to both this

THE REASON FOR WRITING THIS BOOK

EVERYBODY HAS
A TONE THAT YOU CAN FEEL
INTO... THE CODE IS ALL
THAT'S NEEDED.

The Afterlife of J.D. Salinger

and the sorts of antipathy that you feel towards people, too.

Now, in the big picture, there are still those people who don't get along, even in our physically challenged place. However, there's another layer—or perhaps removal of layers—that helps us get to know each other in ways that are more loving. There's a stripping away of perception that alters how you view things. You view things and others with more loving feeling.

That's how it is with everybody here. Everybody sees each other differently, as well as with more lovingkindness, because we're all in this place together for a reason. We're all here to heal.

In your defense—not that you really need one—you have built structures that conform to a way of life that incorporate all sorts of delineations that preclude really getting people on a feeling level—getting them, as in knowing them. You "get them," though, is really more accurate. You sense the way that they choose to be is deeply held in ways that you don't really care about, perhaps. Then when you get to know them, or when you admire them for some reason, your thinking about them shifts. Next, you may find something really lovable about them. The

The Reason for Writing This Book

point is that this feeling you have is always there. You just don't realize it until you change your thinking about something.

This is perhaps the most important thing you can do to be a happy person: to let go of the perceptions that anybody is less than or greater than you or anybody. This is the number one mistake that people make in getting to where you think you need to be. You make so many judgments that you can't really know anything, because why? You're not feeling it.

The reason you do this is to equate your life with something that is solo in scope and not connected, when the reality is that you're indelibly connected with everything around you and everyone all the time. You just forget that sometimes.

So when Holden Caulfield takes aim in his hunter's hat at somebody who he thinks is better off not in his purview, he does what? He imagines it only. He does not take aim, really. In fact, the reason I wrote this was to share how I feel sometimes about some people. There are some people I really would like to see gone from my life, or did when I was alive. But these people serve the vital function of allowing us to review what exactly the world is here to provide us, and in this, it's not going to be perfect. The fact is, it's going to be so much better than perfect that you only have to feel it to know I'm telling the truth.

Perfection is an idea that masks some things that we don't want to see, such as pain and suffering and loss. However, these are perfectly perfect in their imperfection, as the truths that these respectively represent are honor, virtue, and valor. There is honor in pain, there is virtue in suffering, and there is valor in loss. The only things you need to realize is that when you experience these things, it's only a matter of shifting your perspective to realize how heroic you are that makes all the difference.

※

As I said earlier, there's no reason to feel that you're anything less than a soldier of life for just being here in this vacuous, odd place where things don't always make sense. The reason you are here is to make sense enough to feel around for love. That's all you really need to do. If you, in the process, have some fun, then that's really great, too, because fun is important.

The Reason for Writing This Book

THE REASON
YOU ARE HERE IS TO
MAKE SENSE ENOUGH
TO FEEL AROUND
FOR LOVE.

The Afterlife of J.D. Salinger

However, in having fun, you also realize that the fun is always about feeling around and finding the love, and joy is what results. That's the connection being made. That's where the love is.

That's why I'm responding to Mrs. Helfrich's letter: to help her feel into the love for her that I have just in knowing what little I know about her. For I feel her, I sense her, I know her in the deepest ways I can.

How can that be? How can I know anybody else now that I'm dead? The same way you do. The way I described.

※

The reasons that I share this with you is that you are already dead, too. You're as dead as I am, you just haven't realized it yet because there's no reason to. It's not something to fear, either, it's something to realize only. The reason you don't is to solidify what you think into a sound logic so you can realize how bogus it all is and enjoy your life again. Too many hearts are broken in thinking that you have only one life, and that's all over when you die. Stop

The Reason for Writing This Book

this thinking immediately. If you have any reason to be alive, now's the time to live it.

The way I feel now is that to make or break a story, I need to reach into new proclivities of story, and that's how most writers do it. The specialness of this situation demands that I escape from my thinking—even now—to consider how this might occur, and then I gently ease into this new area of exploration with only a bit of trepidation, the same as anybody does with something new. The fact remains that I am I, she is she, but in between are lots of other conditions besides our own. What does she want from me? It is not as easy as it may seem. I don't know what I really have to give her anyway.

When you feel that something urging you into new areas may not be the right thing for you, what do you do? You feel into it, that's what we are saying. That's all.

In my case, she has received the most gracious of talents to heal others through the written word. That's why I am helping her. That's why I have to. That's because I have a similar intent. We are all born with something that each individual—as well as their souls—strive for, and some things that you naturally do. We share an intent of educating people

TOO MANY HEARTS
ARE BROKEN IN THINKING
THAT YOU HAVE ONLY ONE
LIFE, AND THAT'S ALL
OVER WHEN YOU DIE.
STOP THIS THINKING
IMMEDIATELY.

The Reason for Writing This Book

through fiction in ways that really don't matter to most people.

There are many people who really don't care about things that we care about. This is especially true of the Lane Coutells of the world. If you've read *Franny and Zooey*, you know of the character that is somewhat superficial and amiable to a fault.

There's no one who is totally superficial, as there's no one who's totally deep. The difference, really, between people is why they chose to be. The reason to be is to invoke in others something that's important. For us—for Mrs. Helfrich and I—it's the source of the greatest satisfaction for us in that the words mean something, the characters live in the reader, and the jerks of the world respond in shallow ways that record the true nature of some people.

The most important thing that comes from all those words is the chance to make a difference with the individuals who respond enthusiastically to the characters that we love so dearly. In doing this, the world—because of our love for the characters and stories—becomes a bit brighter. The children of the world, especially, have everything to gain from them, because they teach about how much better we might be and how much we can do. In this, the children are the best recipients, because they are the ones who need it the most.

Knowing about people's intent is important because it gets to the point where you just won't be able to connect on a deep level sometimes if you don't really have anything in common besides the superficial things. That's where people get off track: they think too much about the superficial stuff. If they were really wanting something grand, they would go beyond this place—this sort of mechanized world that keeps everything going—and realize that life really does make sense when you feel rather than think, and feeling into people's intent is important. That's what I've learned being here, and it's a forgone conclusion that my work with Mrs. Helfrich is going to be fine because we are soul mates in this respect, as are many individuals who embrace what we are trying to do with our lives.

The Reason for Writing This Book

The reason we say it is going to feel better when you begin to feel at all, or at least more than you do now, is because of our complaints about the world, of course, as well as our desire to break up the sorts of combatant zones of the world. The zones are in each heart, though not external to you. It's something of a stretch to think of combat as anything but on the war fields. However, not every war is fought outside you. Most are inside. And the courage to admit this is why we must say just one more thing about how your partners in spirit can help you.

Take, for example, this occurrence between myself and Mrs. Helfrich. She wants very much to be a writer who is published. There's not anything wrong with this, because that's what all writers want. The purpose for her, therefore, is to be a good writer, to expertly demonstrate her skills.

She has loved my work for many years now. She does not want to completely forgo the sorts of things that I write about: love, mystical knowledge, preaching sometimes (I know I did, however, she loves it too, the preaching). The signs were all there. Her work was somewhat close in tone to mine all along. Why? Because she loved me so much that she incorporated my feeling tone into her work.

The Afterlife of J.D. Salinger

You do this all the time. You love others, you hate others, and in the feeling of both hate and love is the point here: you expertly draw into you each of those types of love when you create things in the lives you lead now. When you hate, it's just love, and when you love, you also hate things, too. The two can't be separated. So if you are feeling blue, realize there's something of a partner there for you to feel into to help you feel better. That's all.

※

The purpose, therefore, of love is to help you sustain yourself so you can happily go about your business. There's not anything much more to this. It's a sense you have that everything's okay, whether you're doing the laundry or climbing Mount Kilimanjaro. The work you do is fueled by love all the time: you just need to be open to it.

The reason we decided to do this with Mrs. Helfrich is to help others to feel better.

That's all. Just feel better.

I promise you with everything that I feel now—which is a great big heart full of love for everybody

The Reason for Writing This Book

in the world trying to make it through each day without feeling terrible about anything—that I will be in your thoughts, helping whenever you want me to be.

I have the sense I can help you now more than I did in my books because this is true: I am here in spite of everything that you may think about the afterlife. I am present in each of your hearts. You can count on me to help you to where you need to be.

Just feel better about everything. Don't over-worry about what you have accomplished. Just do what feels right and It—the Great Being Who, I promise, exists—will take care of the rest. I know because I have the sense that if He or She can be here for me, He or She can be here for anybody.

Love to you all,

Jerome David Salinger
From beyond what you have ever imagined